WEST VIRGINIA

by
Arnout Hyde, Jr.

Robin's Plantain.

CONTENTS

COPYRIGHT 1980 by ARNOUT HYDE, JR.
ALL RIGHTS RESERVED

ISBN 0-9604590-0-6 Hardbound
ISBN 0-9604590-1-4 Limited Edition

LIBRARY OF CONGRESS CATALOG CARD NUMBER 80-82049
First printing 1980
Second printing 1981

Published by Arnout Hyde, Jr.
PRINTED IN THE UNITED STATES OF AMERICA

Sherwood Lake,
Greenbrier County

SUMMER

Canaan Valley
State Park

F A L L

Daybreak Audra State Park, Middle Fork River.

9

W I N T E R

Farm panorama in southern part of state.

Preface

ONE NIGHT WHILE SITTING AROUND A CAMPFIRE ON SHAVER'S FORK SOME YEARS AGO, A COMPANION REMARKED, "ARNOUT, WHY NOT PUBLISH A BOOK OF YOUR PHOTOGRAPHY?" Over the years, I have received letters from WONDERFUL WEST VIRGINIA subscribers asking if a collection of my work was available. Encouraged by these suggestions, serious planning began on a book. After stirring many ideas together, I finalized on the theme of the four seasons. So much of our environment revolves about spring, summer, fall and winter. What West Virginian doesn't look forward to spring planting, warm summer evenings, autumn's show of color and winter's first snowfall?

Since this is a photographic book, prime consideration was given to the selection of pictures. It was thought that readers would enjoy seeing a few favorite previously published scenes, however, the majority of the pictures are new, unseen work. The choice of subjects with descriptive copy presented some difficult decisions. Let me explain; West Virginia as we know is blessed with much God-given beauty, numerous historic locations and the best of people. In the scope of this book it would be impossible to include all topics and locations. I have tried to include those subjects thought to be of general interest.

I have held a unique position during the last ten years in working for the Department of Natural Resources and assisting in producing the popular State Magazine WONDERFUL WEST VIRGINIA. Not only has it been a privilege to work with its outstanding editor Ed Johnson, but a real opportunity has been mine to assist in modestly proclaiming the beauty of our state through this publication.

Most of the photography in my book was done on weekends and vacations while traveling backroads with a four-wheel vehicle and backpacking on in where the roads ended. Canoe trips accounted for many of the stream and water photos. A high wing, single-engine Cessna plane with an open window was slowed to 60 mph for aerial views.

Perhaps of interest to some readers would be the photo equipment I use. While a G.I. stationed in Germany, I photographed free-lance jobs to earn money to buy German cameras and equipment. The camera I use the most is a 4 by 5 inch Linhof, a relatively heavy camera with an assortment of lenses and most generally a heavy tripod. This camera produces a 4 by 5 inch color transparency from which the printer makes a set of negatives called a separation and this is used in the final four-color printing process. The combined camera equipment I use weighs 35 pounds and is carried in a backpack which was adapted by fitting foam rubber as cushioning. Other cameras are also used. For instance, a Nikon underwater 35 mm is great for raft trips. I learned the hard way when an upset canoe on New River damaged some expensive gear.

The book has been a new and fascinating experience from the standpoint of editing, layout, learning the printing process and writing copy.

I would like to acknowledge persons that helped me directly and indirectly with this publication. My wonderful wife and companion, Teresa, accompanied me on many photo trips, walking and climbing over West Virginia terrain and camping through many a rainy night waiting for a clear photo day. Her supportive help and love throughout the project will always be appreciated. Lucia Katherine, our three year old daughter, willingly posed for some of the pictures in the book. My father, Arnout Hyde Sr., researched and wrote much of the copy and offered assistance through all phases of the work. Without doubt the best public relations person and devoted supporter one could have must be my dear mother, Katherine Hardy Hyde. Ed Johnson is a valued friend from whom I've learned much. Our association has been an educational and rewarding experience I cherish. The Department of Natural Resources is a state agency I am justifiably proud to be a part of. It is an organization which is comprised of dedicated professionals whom I believe give West Virginia and its citizens a leadership in preserving our natural resources. Osbra Eye offered his extensive knowledge as a botanist in identifying many of the wildflower pictures. Minnie Powell, the best of friends, typed the manuscript. The following persons offered assistance and suggestions: David Bice, George Davis, Bob Dittmar, Darrell Jessee, and Steve and Marialice Seaman.

Wolfe Creek, Fayette County.

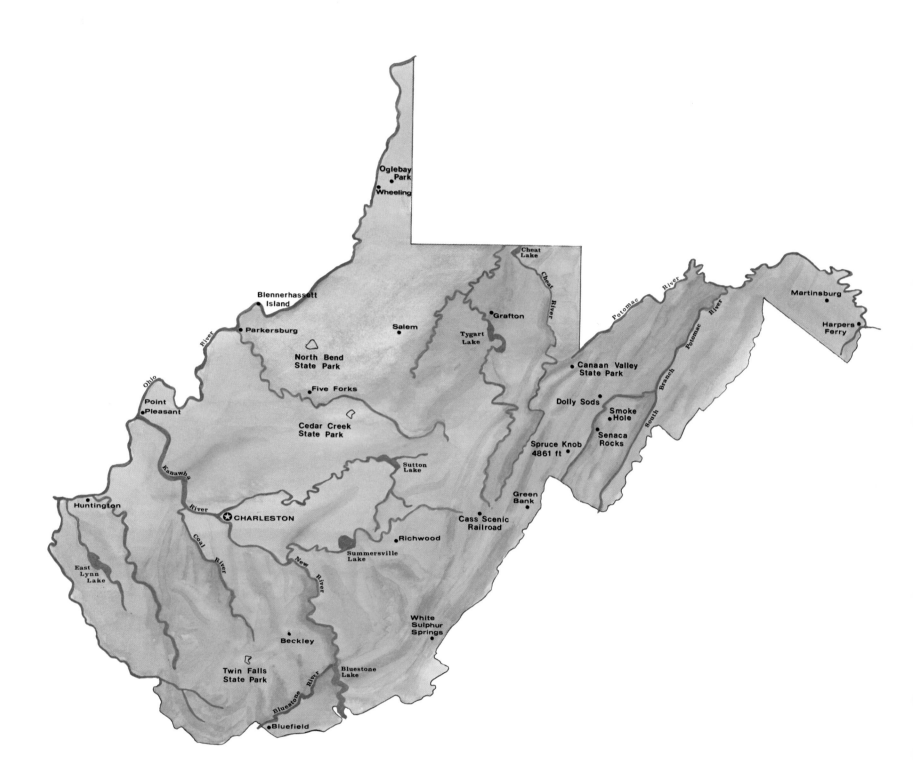

Oglebay
Park

Wheeling

Cheat
Lake

Blennerhassett
Island

Martinsburg

Grafton

Potomac River

Salem

Harpers
Ferry

Parkersburg

River

Tygart
Lake

Cheat River

North Bend
State Park

Canaan Valley
State Park

Ohio

Five Forks

Dolly Sods

Smoke
Hole

Point
Pleasant

Cedar Creek
State Park

South Branch

Senaca
Rocks

Spruce Knob
4861 ft

Sutton
Lake

Kanawha

Huntington

River

Green
Bank

CHARLESTON

Cass Scenic
Railroad

Coal River

Richwood

East
Lynn
Lake

Summersville
Lake

New River

White
Sulphur
Springs

Beckley

Twin Falls
State Park

Bluestone
Lake

Bluestone River

Bluefield

MAP DESIGNED EXCLUSIVELY FOR THIS BOOK BY
HEIDI M. ROUB

West Virginia Highlights

State Motto: Montani Semper Liberi (Mountaineers Are Always Free)
Location: In the Appalachian Region: Bordering States, Virginia, Maryland,
                      Pennsylvania, Ohio, and Kentucky
Area: 24,181 square miles, including 111 square miles of water area,
                      41st in size among the states
Elevation: Highest: Spruce Knob (Pendleton County) 4,862 feet above sea
                      level
                      Lowest: Harpers Ferry (Jefferson County) 247 feet above sea level
Population: 1970 census, 1,744,237
                      1980 estimated, 1,846,169
                      61% rural, 39% urban, density 72 persons per square mile
Government: *Congress:* U.S. senators, 2; U.S. representatives, 4
                      Electoral Votes: 6; *State Legislature:* senators, 34; delegates, 100
                      Counties: 55
Capital: Charleston
Statehood: June 20, 1863 the 35th state
State Bird: Cardinal
State Flower: Rhododendron
State Tree: Sugar Maple
State Animal   Black Bear
Chief Products: *Agriculture:* milk, turkeys, eggs, apples, beef cattle, chickens
                      Manufacturing: chemicals, primary metals, fabricated metal prod-
                                       ucts, stone, clay and glass products, nonelectric
                                       machinery
                      Mining: coal, petroleum, natural gas, natural gas liquids, sand and
                                gravel
National Forests: Monongahela, Jefferson and George Washington totaling one million
                      acres
State Parks: 33 totaling 65,000 acres
State Forests: 9 totaling 77,000 acres
Public Hunting Areas: 36

Left—Blooming rhododendron.
Top—Fawn surveys its surroundings in Boone County.

THE GREENBRIER

The Springhouse

THE GREENBRIER, WEST VIRGINIA'S PREMIER SOCIAL RESORT, IS WELL KNOWN THROUGHOUT THE WORLD. IT HAS BEEN A PLAYGROUND FOR MANY YEARS FOR PRESIDENTS, BUSINESS TYCOONS, wealthy planters and foreign dignitaries, as well as the general public. The motto, "Life as it should be," finds full expression on the resort's 6500 acres developed to suit virtually every taste.

The site of The Greenbrier came into prominence over two hundred years ago when a sulfur water spring was thought to have curative powers for many ailments. In 1778 a woman named Amanda Anderson is said to have made a remarkable recovery from crippling rheumatism after immersion in the spring water. Word of the spring's powers spread and over the years popularity of the area grew until in time the simple rental cabins gave way to development that became a spa. It was not long before social life accompanied "taking the waters" and a splendid resort came into being. It became popular among wealthy southern planters to build cottages around the spring and in time a two story tavern with accomodations for 60 guests was built.

Over the years resort buildings were enlarged, remodeled, torn down and rebuilt until today's magnificent estate evolved. Whereas today the resort is dedicated to man's pleasure it has had grim periods during wars. It changed hands between the North and South during the Civil War with each side using it as a military hospital. At the start of World War II it housed enemy diplomatic personnel until exchanges could be effected. After that it became a military hospital. At war's end the Chesapeake & Ohio Railway Company repurchased the property and returned it to private resort status.

Today the complex includes a hotel with 650 rooms, three 18 hole golf courses, 20 tennis courts, 2 olympicsized swimming pools, 8 bowling lanes, stables and an outstanding diagnostic health clinic. Other attractions include a theatre, gun club, exclusive shops and an arts colony.

Tulips enhance the north entrance.

Top—Aerial view of The Greenbrier.
Bottom—The Greenbrier's lakeside golf course.

Meadow Creek, Greenbrier County

Left—Hang glider soars off Flat Top Mountain.
Bottom—Boardwalk through Cranberry Glades, Pocahontas County.

Anna Reeves Jarvis,
Anna's mother.

Anna M. Jarvis

Andrews Methodist Episcopal Church

MOTHER'S DAY SHRINE

WEST VIRGINIA IS THE PROUD BIRTHPLACE OF ANNA JARVIS, SPONSOR OF MOTHER'S DAY, A CUSTOM NOW CELEBRATED THROUGHOUT THE CIVILIZED world. She was born on May 1, 1864 and received her primary and secondary education in the Grafton, West Virginia schools. After attending Mary Baldwin College in Staunton, Virginia, she taught in Grafton schools for seven years.

On the death of her father, the family moved to Philadelphia, Pennsylvania, where her mother died in 1905. Two years later, Anna invited friends to join in commemorating her mother's death. She chose the second Sunday in May and suggested that white carnations be worn. This flower was selected because to her it represented purity and was also her mother's favorite.

The next year Miss Jarvis wrote to officials of the Andrews Methodist Episcopal Church in Grafton suggesting that all mothers be honored. The church complied on May 10, 1908 and has celebrated this day ever since. West Virginia Governor William E. Glasscock issued a Mother's Day proclamation on April 26, 1910. This was followed in 1914 by a joint resolution of Congress which established the second Sunday in May as Mother's Day. This was approved by President Woodrow Wilson.

Miss Jarvis died in Philadelphia on November 24, 1948. She left a legacy, however, that will live forever. The Andrews Methodist Episcopal Church has become the Mother's Day Shrine.

*Top—Carnations grace inside Mother's Day Shrine.
Bottom—Aerial view of Mother's Day Shrine located in
Grafton.*

Left—Dame's Rocket.
Top—Young bobcat.
Left bottom—Large flowered trillium.

STATE PARKS

THE WEST VIRGINIA STATE PARK SYSTEM HAS GROWN FROM A MODEST BEGINNING IN 1925 UNTIL TODAY IT RATES AS ONE OF THE FINEST IN THE NATION. THE FACT THAT THIS CAME ABOUT IN A STATE not one of the giants in size, population and personal wealth is a tribute to its farsighted people and government. The 1925 Legislature created a State Forest, Park and Conservation Commission for the purpose of studying development of these resources. The concept grew into reality over the years along with changes in law and administrative bodies until today the far-flung system is run exceptionally well by the Department of Natural Resources.

By any standard the park system today must be considered diverse, catering to a wide range of tastes. One can choose between primitive wilderness camping or a fully developed trailer site; a pioneer-type rustic cabin or plush resort-like lodge or cabin; the department even runs a full-scale railroad (Cass).

During the 1930's the Civilian Conservation Corps (C.C.C.) contributed a great deal to the early development of the park system. They built a number of stone structures and log cabins which are still in use today. The program was supervised by the National Park Service with state assistance.

West Virginia is justly proud of its park system.

Top—Water powered grist mill in operation at Babcock State Park.
Left—Aerial view of Pipestem State Park.
Bottom—Swimming pool at Lost River State Park.

Top—Rural scene looking towards George Washington National Forest in Pendleton County.
Left—Historic Coleman Chapel in Jackson County.
Bottom—Covered bridge spans Tygart River at Phillippi, site of the first land battle of the Civil War.

NATIONAL RADIO ASTRONOMY OBSERVATORY

THE NATIONAL RADIO ASTRONOMY OB-SERVATORY, OPERATED BY ASSOCIATED UNIVERSITIES INCORPORATED, UNDER CONTRACT WITH THE NATIONAL SCIENCE FOUNDATION, IS LOCATED IN THE Deer Creek Valley near Green Bank, West Virginia. The purpose of the Observatory is, in a broad sense, to add to man's knowledge of the universe. Specifically, radio astronomers study the universe by collecting and measuring radio waves emitted by celestial matter. Although scientists have been aware of radio waves from outer space for many years, it has only been pursued seriously for the past fifty years. Radio signals from outer space were measured for the first time by Karl Jansky of the Bell Telephone Laboratories in 1930. He built an antenna which could be steered in any direction to study radio noise generated in the earth's atmosphere. His interest was in noise interference with a projected transatlantic radio telephone system. His studies identified radio waves emitted by our galaxy. This was the birth of radio astronomy. A replica of Jansky's antenna has been built and installed on the north side of the Observatory entrance.

Since Jansky's time, a number of highly sophisticated radio telescopes have been built and installed at Green Bank. These are the dish-shaped devices dominating the landscape. They range in size from 45 to 300 feet in diameter, and despite weighing hundreds of tons can be rotated with pinpoint accuracy. Their purpose is to collect and concentrate very weak radio signals from outer space.

The scope and cost of basic research such as that done at Green Bank is too great for a small organization to handle. It requires a consortium of many scientists, institutions and vast amounts of money. This is accomplished through the organizations previously mentioned.

The National Science Foundation is an independent agency of the Federal Government. It has a director and National Scientific Board appointed by the President of the United States. It supports scientific research through grants from funds appropriated by the United States Congress. Typical is the contractual funding of radio astronomy with Associated Universities, Incorporated, a non-profit organization of nine universities; namely, Columbia, Cornell, Harvard, Johns Hopkins, Massachusetts Institute of Technology, Pennsylvania, Princeton, Rochester and Yale.

The research facilities are available to all qualified scientists and findings are not classified, but are made public by publication in technical journals.

The Green Bank area was chosen for the Observatory after an extensive search. Most of modern man's electrical machinery are sources of radio waves and these can interfere with detection of very weak radio astronomical measurements. The Green Bank area was found to be acceptably quiet. A National Radio Quiet Zone was established to preserve this condition. This allows the Observatory a voice in permitting new radio sources in the area. It is further strengthened by agreement with the Federal Communications Commission, Inter-Service Radio Advisory Committee and West Virginia legislation.

Whereas basic research in radio astronomy is the prime objective of the Observatory, everyday practical benefits have been an offshoot. Low radio noise receiving systems developed by the Observatory are now used in medicine, forest fire detection, navigation and earthquake forecasting. No doubt man's understanding of his universe as well as everyday tangible benefits will continue to expand with continued research in radio astronomy.

The 85 foot Howard E. Tatel Telescope, one of the oldest telescopes at the Observatory, was first used in 1959.

Top—The 140 foot telescope, the largest equatorially mounted radio telescope in the world.
Bottom—Aerial view of the National Radio Astronomy Observatory.

Morning mist filled valleys in Tucker County.

Top—*Red trillium.*
Left—*South Fork, South Branch of the Potomac River near Sugar Grove.*
Bottom—*Cranberry River in Nicholas County.*

Aerial scene of the Oglebay Complex.

OGLEBAY

OGLEBAY IS A COMBINATION OF MANY THINGS SKILLFULLY COMBINED ON 1,460 DEVELOPED ACRES. ABOVE ALL IT IS A MONUMENT TO THE PHILAN-THROPY OF COLONEL EARL W. OGLE-bay, who died in 1926 and willed his Waddington Farm to the City of Wheeling. The gift's purpose was to develop a public park for the enjoyment and improvement of life for people of Wheeling and elsewhere.

Through untiring efforts of Chrispin Oglebay, nephew of Earl, the Wheeling Park Commission and many others, Oglebay has developed into an institution of wide repute. It is much more than a city park.

Educational and cultural pursuits are many and varied. The original mansion houses a museum which displays an early colonial kitchen, antique firearms, a fabulous glassware collection and the "Declaration of Independence of West Virginia," to name a few of its treasures. An outdoor theatre seating 3,000 schedules many enlightening performances. Outstanding horticultural achievements include greenhouses, gardens, arboretum and landscaping.

The park offers golf, swimming, tennis, lakes, horseback riding, picnic sites, skiing, lodge and cabins and a Children's Center. Of special interest in the Children's Center Area is the Good Children's Zoo. This 65-acre area includes appropriate buildings, exhibits and a wide range of animals, some of which can be petted.

The City of Wheeling is fortunate to have the Oglebay Complex which has hosted so many visitors.

Lucia Katherine's first pony ride at the Good Children's Zoo.

Top—Tulips bloom at Oglebay.
Bottom—Boaters enjoy Schenk Lake at Oglebay.

Chris Taylor tries his luck on a trout stream.

S
U
M
M
E
R

Top—Robert Taylor splashes rocks at the Zenith Mill in Monroe County.
Top left—The Forks of Cheat Baptist Church near Morgantown founded in 1775.
Bottom—Fisherman enjoys the solitude of early dawn on Sherwood Lake.

Top—Natural stone arch in Big Ugly Public Hunting area, Lincoln County.
Left—Goose Creek, Ritchie County.

DOLLY SODS

DOLLY SODS, LIKE THE MYTHICAL BIRD, PHOENIX, OF ANCIENT EGYPTIAN SUN WORSHIP, ROSE TO NEW LIFE FROM ITS ASHES. BEFORE THE TURN OF THE CENTURY, THE AREA WE NOW call Dolly Sods was densely forested largely in red spruce. The forest floor was deep in humus that had accumulated over many years.

Removal of the trees by timbering allowed full impact of the sun to reach the ground and dry what had been moist organic matter. This plus the slash left from lumbering combined to produce a combustible mix which caught fire and burned to bare ground, except where a few swampy areas afforded protection. Many of the original native plants have survived and prospered. The botany is similar to that to be found in parts of Canada.

Portions of four West Virginia counties, Tucker, Grant, Randolph and Pendleton make up the Dolly Sods area. It is high country with elevations in the 3000 to 4000-foot level, generally exceeded, however, by neighboring 4862-foot Spruce Knob, the highest point in the State.

Dolly Sods offers varied pursuits of an outdoor nature. Despite the cruel fall and winter weather hunting is popular. The name "Roaring Plain" has been used for the area and this says something about the prevailing wind which is so strong and persistent from the west that nothing develops on that side of the trees—they have a three-sided appearance.

Those interested in botany will recognize predominance of the heath family making up the vegetation. These include rhododendrons, azaleas, mountain laurel, cranberries, blueberries and huckleberries to name a few. Blueberries and huckleberries are the most numerous plants and draw many pickers, both man and animal, during July and August when their fruits are ripe. Rattlesnakes and copperheads are quite common and present a hazard of which knowledgeable pickers are well aware.

There is no easy way to describe Dolly Sods except to say it is unique. The gifted writer and botanist Maurice Brooks aptly applies the term "biologic wealth" in his descriptive writings.

The Nature Conservancy recently purchased almost 16,000 acres of Dolly Sods mineral rights and transferred them to the United States Forest Service. This outstanding public service assures future generations perpetuation of this unique area.

Timber Rattlesnake.

Dolly Sods.

Left—Blooming mountain laurel on Dolly Sods.
Bottom—Gaudineer scenic area, a remnant of a vast virgin spruce forest, in the Monogahela National Forest.

POINT PLEASANT

POINT PLEASANT, LOCATED WHERE THE KANAWHA JOINS THE OHIO RIVER, TO-DAY OBSERVES A BUSY SCENE OF WATER TRANSPORTATION. A LITTLE OVER TWO HUNDRED YEARS EARLIER, THE SCENE WAS DIFferent. A battle was fought there between Colonial troops under the command of Colonel Andrew Lewis and the Federated Indian tribes under Chief Cornstalk. Whereas the military outcome was somewhat indecisive, many historians find major significance in the claim that it was the first battle of the Revolutionary War. The United States Congress lent status to this claim in 1908 by the wording of an appropriation bill authorizing funds to be used in erecting a monument at the battle site.

The frontier lands beyond the Virginia borders were in dispute by several factions at that time. The Colonials were seeking new homesteads to settle, the British were concerned about encroachment into territories supporting their lucrative fur trade, and the Indians were protecting their homeland. The Battle of Point Pleasant was a result of British encouraged Indian massacres of pioneer settlers.

A park, museum and imposing granite monument commemorating this historic event now grace the battle site. Success of this venture is largely due to the efforts of the Daughters of the American Revolution (DAR).

Right—Historic monument at Tu-Endie-Wei Park.
Bottom—Point Pleasant at the confluence of the Ohio and the Kanawha rivers.

Pastoral scene of the South Branch of the Potomac River in the Moorefield vicinity.

Left—Rural view of Red Sulphur Springs, Monroe County.
Top—Country road in Holly River State Park, Webster County.

CASS

A VISIT TO THE TOWN OF CASS AND ITS RAIL-ROAD IS APT TO BRING VIVID MEMORIES TO THOSE OLD ENOUGH TO REMEMBER THE EARLY YEARS OF THIS CENTURY AND ITS LUMBERING INDUSTRY. Younger folks will see where, and to some extent, how that industry operated. The machine shops, railway station, and mill buildings were intact until a few years ago when they were lost to fire. The railroad and much of the original rolling stock have been revived and are in use today hauling passengers. The passenger cars were converted from the original log carriers.

During the summer months thousands of persons ride the trains daily over the original logging routes to the first terminal, Whittaker Station, or the full distance to Bald Knob, the second highest peak in West Virginia; elevation 4842 feet. The steep grade, as high as 10%, requires 4½ hours to travel the 11 miles from Cass to Bald Knob. It is an experience never to be forgotten.

When railroads were used, the steep grades encounted by the mountainous logging operations required specialized equipment.

Late in the 19th century locomotives were developed which could negotiate the grades. The basic principle employed gear reduction drive to every wheel of both engine and tender. In this way enormous traction was accomplished and a single wheel could not slip under a heavy load as was common with conventional locomotives. Shay and Climax were the most common locomotives of this type used in West Virginia. Shay engines are used on the Cass Railroad today.

Before the mill burned, it was possible to recreate the path of log to finished lumber. Logs reaching the mill by trainload were discharged into a pond bordering the tracks and mill. When needed, the logs were floated to a cleated chain drive incline which carried them up into the mill and on to a sloping feed ramp for discharge to the saw carriage. Logs rolled from the ramp onto a carriage, which in turn carried them to a large band saw. The boards cut by repetitive passes were transferred to other parts of the mill by roller conveyors. Here the lumber was sorted, graded and further directed to its various uses.

During its heyday Cass had a population of about 2000. The town had schools, churches, restaurants, saloons, more than 400 houses and a large company store known as the Pocahontas Supply Company. The store served the needs of the town, logging camps and surrounding countryside. The store building today serves as a restaurant, gift shop and museum.

The early lumbering industry is now preserved as a working historical monument under the auspices of a state park named Cass.

Left—Old shops at Cass prior to 1972 fire.
Top—Mighty Shay Engine climbs mountain grade at Bald Mountain.
Overleaf—Night scene of Shay Engines at the Cass Station.

Top—Rare photograph showing the original lumber company shops in use by Cass Railroad before 1972 fire.
Bottom—Aerial view of Cass.

Leatherbark Creek near Cass.

Top—Mountain view from Route 72 in Tucker County.
Right—Bluestone Lake, Summers County.
Bottom—Sunset in public hunting and fishing area, Pocahontas County.

Top—Rafting through New River Canyon.
Right—Raft plows into turbulent whitewater on the New River.

NEW RIVER

THE NEW RIVER IN WEST VIRGINIA HAS ENJOYED A SURGE OF POPULARITY DURING THE PAST DECADE ALONG WITH RECOGNITION AND APPRECIATION OF ITS HISTORY, SCENIC AND RECREATION POtential. A number of persons have worked hard to preserve that section of the river and its gorge from Hinton to Fayetteville. This majestic area has aptly been described as the "Grand Canyon of the East."

The United States Congress has assured development consistent with its beauty, archeology, geology and recreation potential by inclusion of these 52 miles of river and gorge in the National Park and Recreation Act of 1978. The New River Gorge National River is the tenth river to be included in the National Park System.

The name "New River" is certainly a misnomer inasmuch as the stream is the oldest in North America and estimated to be one hundred million years old. The New River originates in North Carolina, flows through Virginia and into West Virginia where it ends by joining the Gauley at Gauley Bridge to form the Kanawha River.

The white water sport of floating turbulent streams in rafts, canoes and kayaks has become popular in recent years. The New River Gorge has been described as one of the nation's most extensive concentrations of white water with its 21 major rapids in 15 miles, some of which are rated No. 5. Difficulty in negotiating rapids is rated on a scale of one to six with No. 6 considered almost unmanageable, or traversed with utmost difficulty and danger to life. Thousands of persons enjoy the beauty and thrill of raft trips through the gorge each summer with the majority carried by skilled commercial rafters.

Coal mining developed rapidly in the gorge area during the early 1900's and with it the inevitable boom towns. The most famous or notorious, depending on your point of view, was Thurmond. In its heyday it was known as the "Dodge City of the East" with a significant portion of the population of 500 numbered among adventurers of both sexes. Legend has it that a poker game lasted for 14 years in one of the hotels.

We West Virginians, as well as the rest of the nation, are fortunate that the majestic New River Gorge National River will now be preserved for posterity.

Top—View of New River from Grandview State Park.
Right—Sun sets on the New River Canyon.
Bottom—Sun silhouettes rafters on the New River.

DURING THE PAST SEVERAL DECADES, ATTENTION HAS FOCUSED ON ECONOMIC DEVELOPMENT PROBLEMS IN THE APPALACHIAN REGION OF OUR NATION. THE MOUNTAINOUS TERRAIN, while beautiful and a mountaineer's pride, presents formidable obstacles. Interstate and corridor highways are planned to alleviate the problems by making West Virginia and the rest of Appalachia more available to the rest of the nation. Corridor "L" connecting interstates 79 and 77 crosses the New River Canyon near Fayette Station. This crossing spawned the famous New River Gorge Bridge.

It is hard to discuss this bridge without using superlatives. We are told it is one of the highest above water and one of the longest arched suspension bridges in the world. The tons of steel and cubic yards of concrete used stagger the imagination. We are accustomed to the painting of bridges in a never-ending struggle against rust and corrosion. Such an enormously expensive task has been eliminated for this bridge by the use of a corrosion-resistant type of steel, the brown color of which is due

NEW RIVER GORGE BRIDGE

to a protective oxidation process.

The bridge height of nearly 900 feet above the river required unusual construction methods. Construction was literally from the air down rather than from the ground up. Two 330-foot high towers were constructed on each rim of the canyon and cableways suspended between them. Trolleys, capable of carrying the heavy steel segments, transported the pieces on the cableways to their respective positions where they were bolted in place. On May 13, 1976 the last two pieces of the arch were installed thus completing a major phase of the job.

One can imagine the collective sighs of relief when the last section was fastened and the strength of the massive structure was assured. It was a memorable occasion drawing dignitaries from throughout the state and nation.

Viewing facilities were built by the Department of Natural Resources which allowed visitors to watch construction. This soon became a popular tourist attraction. The New River Gorge Bridge was officially opened on October 22, 1977.

Colonial bread.

THE TOWN OF SALEM TRACES ITS ORIGIN TO THE LATE 1700'S WHEN DISSENSION OVER REVOLUTIONARY WAR LOYALTIES SPLIT THE SHREWSBURY SEVENTH DAY BAPTIST CHURCH OF SALEM, NEW Jersey. A part of the congregation, consisting of ten families, migrated to what was then known as western Virginia. Their final settlement was on Ten Mile Creek in what is now Harrison County, and this they named "New Salem."

Life in New Salem was typical of pioneers in the wilderness areas of America at that time. Survival depended on endless work, ingenuity and skills to supply food, shelter, clothing and other necessities of life. Their church was a source of strength and inspiration, and offered a means of community gathering.

Buildings were constructed of logs from the vast forests. Wood from these trees also served for fuel as well as furniture and many household utensils. Food came from hunting, crops grown on arduously cleared land and edible items growing wild. Animal skins and "linsey-woolsey," a course cloth spun and woven from

Reconstructed buildings at Fort New Salem.

SALEM

wool and flax, grown and processed by the pioneers, served in large part for clothing.

The community grew in a normal fashion and during 1905 the town was incorporated and the name shortened to Salem.

Salem College under John Randolph's direction has been active in preserving our early heritage, a major undertaking of which has been the building of Fort New Salem. The buildings in the complex are authentic early structures donated by residents of the area. Each building was taken apart at its original location and faithfully reassembled at the fort.

When visiting the numerous buildings which now serve as museums, workshops and classrooms, where early crafts are taught, the imagination roams. It is easy to imagine at least a portion of pioneer life. Craftsmen plying early trades are dressed in the garb of the period. Wood smoke from the chimneys lends a pleasant odor outside and foretells the scene inside before the fireplace where cooking or quilting may be seen.

The reconstruction and teachings at Fort New Salem are a remarkable achievement and will do much to sustain a faith in our heritage.

Early printing.

Re-enactment of colonial times at Fort New Salem.

Top—Butterflies on butterfly weeds.
Following overleaf—Evening landscape near Petersburg.
Bottom—Sunset in Pocahontas County.

Top left—Deer posed in North Bend State Park, Ritchie County.
Bottom left—Tree lined street in Alderson.
Top right—Floating leaves on the Cacapon River.
Bottom right—Boys play football along country road, Wyoming County.

F
A
L
L

HARPERS FERRY

HARPERS FERRY, GIVEN NATIONAL MONUMENT STATUS BY CONGRESS IN 1944, IS CURRENTLY UNDERGOING RESTORATION OF ITS MANY HISTORIC LANDMARKS. IT IS SITUATED on a narrow, rocky tongue of land in Jefferson County at the confluence of the Shenandoah and Potomac rivers. The view from the cliffs overlooking the joining of the rivers is spectacular. It is at this point that Thomas Jefferson is quoted as saying the view was "worth a voyage across the Atlantic." From this point one can see three states: Maryland across the Potomac River, Virginia across the Shenandoah River, and West Virginia to one's back.

Harpers Ferry is a popular tourist attraction where history buffs may easily trace the events so well chronicled in textbooks. The National Park Service is restoring many of the old buildings and the overall atmosphere of the area. Future generations will continue to enjoy this part of our national heritage.

Harpers Ferry, while rich in history, has had a full share of strife and tragedy due to war and floods.

In 1735, Robert Harper purchased from Lord Fairfax for 60 guineas (about $300) the land which ultimately became the general area of Harpers Ferry. The industrial potential of the area was later recognized because of its proximity to the capital at Washington. The rivers furnished transportation and power. Raw materials, such as iron ore, coal and forests, were important ingredients of an armaments industry. George Washington recognized this and the Congress authorized an arsenal to be built in 1796.

Early morning view from Maryland Heights of Harpers Ferry situated at the confluence of the Shenandoah and Potomac rivers.

Top—Brown, at Kennedy Farm, planning raid on U.S. Arsenal.
Bottom—Stagecoach Inn built 1826-34.

The armory played an important part in arming a fledgling nation reaching its zenith and demise at the start of the Civil War. Although the armory was destroyed, the area had strategic importance throughout the war years because of its access to Washington and the Shenandoah Valley. Of further importance was completion of the Chesapeake and Ohio Canal from the capital to Cumberland. The Baltimore and Ohio Railroad was also built about the same time and parallelled the canal for much of its distance. The canal was unable to compete with the railroad and to recover from flood damage so in time it was abandoned.

Early in the Civil War, Confederate troops marched on Harpers Ferry, and the Union forces, being outnumbered, were forced to retreat after first burning the arsenal. The Confederates, however, were able to salvage much of the strategic machinery which was put to use in their armories in Virginia and North Carolina. The area changed hands several more times before the war ended and each time major destruction took place.

Despite the fact that Harpers Ferry played an important role in the nation's progress prior to the Civil War, it probably is best remembered because of John Brown's famous raid on the armory.

During the summer of 1859 John Brown, an active slavery abolitionist, set up headquarters on the Kennedy Farm in Maryland. He used the name Isaac Smith and claimed to be prospecting for minerals in the area. During the night of October 16, 1859 along with 22 followers, he marched on and captured the armory and town of Harpers Ferry. By noon of the next day, militia companies from Charles Town, Martinsburg, Shepherdstown, Winchester and other areas surrounded the town, and Brown's men retreated to the engine house. That night, Colonel Robert E. Lee and Lieutenant J. E. B. Stuart arrived from Washington with 90 marines. At daybreak Brown's fort was stormed and taken. Brown and six of his men were captured, ten were killed and five escaped. Brown was tried and convicted in Charles Town of murder and treason on November 2, 1859 and hanged on December 2, 1859.

Top—Harpers Ferry with John Brown's Fort in foreground. The Armory Fire
Engine House was used by Brown during his abortive raid.
Following overleaf—Dawn on Shenandoah Street.
Bottom—U.S. Marines subduing Brown's raiders in Armory Fire Engine House.

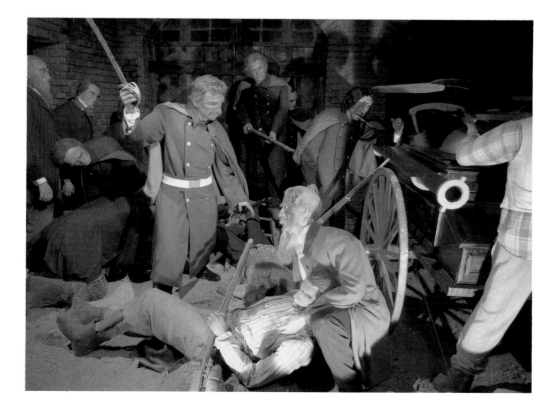

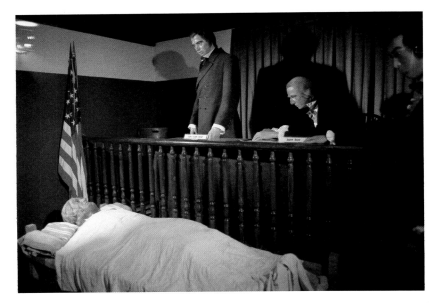

Top—Brown, recovering from sword wounds, during his trial at Charles Town.
Right—Daybreak over Shenandoah River at Harpers Ferry.
Bottom—Brown pauses on gallow steps.

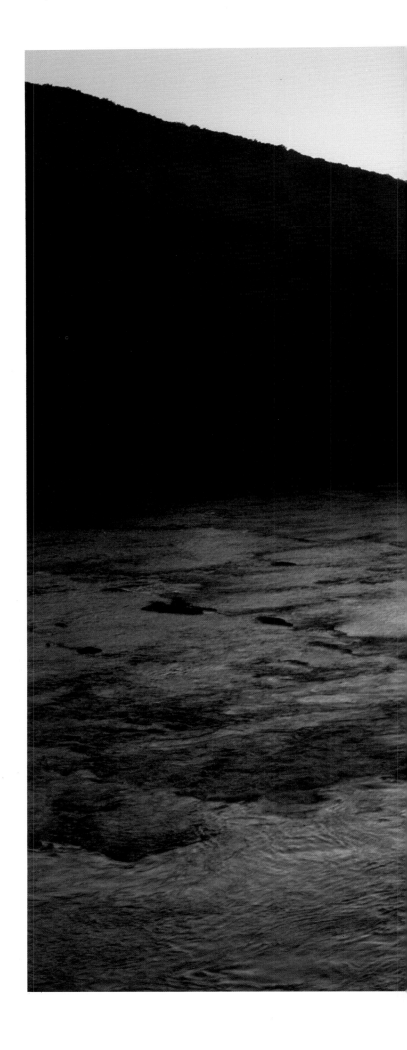

Left—Rural scene from Route 219 near Slatyfork.
Top—Bolivar Heights, Jefferson County.

Evening aerial view of Blennerhassett Island on the Ohio Rver.

BLENNERHASSETT ISLAND

BLENNERHASSETT ISLAND, A LAND MASS OF ABOUT 500 ACRES, WAS FORMED IN PREHISTORIC TIMES BY THE DEPOSIT OF GLACIAL DEBRIS. IT IS LOCATED IN THE OHIO RIVER TWO MILES DOWNSTREAM from Parkersburg.

The area is rich in history. Extensive archeological studies have recovered numerous artifacts and established the presence of man as early as 12,000 B.C. Blennerhassett Island is best known, however, because of its relatively recent history of the early nineteenth century involving Aaron Burr.

Harmon Blennerhassett, a wealthy aristocrat, was socially ostracized in England after marrying a young niece. He and his bride came to America to reestablish their lives and social position. They lived for short periods in New York and Philadelphia and ultimately in Pittsburgh. From here they started by keelboat down the Ohio River in search of a suitable site on which to build a plantation. He purchased 170 acres at the upper end of what was then called Bachus Island, located in the Ohio River. Blannerhassett completed a beautiful mansion by 1800 and for some years entertained lavishly, thus regaining social position. Life was happy here until the appearance of Aaron Burr.

Aaron Burr, a brilliant, ambitious lawyer-politician, was defeated for the United States Presidency by Thomas Jefferson. He was also defeated for the governorship of New York. Bitterness in the campaign resulted in Burr challenging Alexander Hamilton to a duel in which Hamilton was killed. Burr was in political disfavor as a result, and like Blennerhassett, sought to reestablish his position in the West.

Blennerhassett and Burr met and friendship led to a scheme to establish an empire in the southwestern lands then owned by Spain. Word of the plot reached President Jefferson who sent militia to arrest the conspirators. They were arrested in Natchez, Mississippi, and Burr was tried and acquitted in Richmond, Virginia. Blennerhassett was never brought to trial.

The mansion was looted by the militia and later accidentally burned by a slave. Blennerhassett died a broken man on the Isle of Guernsey during 1831.

On September 7, 1972, Blennerhassett Island was listed in the National Register of Historic Places and that same year the West Virginia Legislature created the Blennerhassett Island Historical Commission.

Right—Evening farm scene in Webster County.
Bottom left—Glen Ferris Hydroelectric Power Plant at Kanawha Falls.
Bottom right—Country scene near French Creek.

Top—Cheat River Canyon as seen from Coopers Rock State Forest overlook.
Right—Seneca Lake in Seneca State Forest.

STATE FORESTS

AT THE PRESENT TIME THERE ARE NINE STATE FORESTS LOCATED IN TEN COUNTIES OF WEST VIRGINIA. COOPERS ROCK, 12,748 ACRES, IN MONONGALIA AND PRESTON COUNTIES IS THE LARGEST AND Greenbrier, 5,062 acres, in Greenbrier County is the smallest. The combined acreage of the nine forests is 76,863: Seneca State Forest in Pocahontas County is the oldest, started in 1924 with the invaluable aid of the Civilian Conservation Corps (C.C.C.).

The Code of West Virginia defines the purpose of the State Forests to be for ''growing timber, demonstrating forestry, furnishing or protecting watersheds or providing public recreation.'' In fulfilling this mandate, the Department of Natural Resources does a creditable job of balancing all feasible uses of the land. Most tracts of land, as originally acquired, were in poor condition due to uncontrolled timbering practices and fires. Good forestry management has returned most of the land to productivity with a steady increase in timber harvest.

Wildlife, vegetation, soil, streams and water quality have all benefitted by return of the trees. This, in turn, has made a wide range of recreation pursuits available to man. Hunting, fishing, camping, hiking and other outdoor activities are enjoyed by many. The present management practice demonstrates that the forests can serve many uses in harmony and that timber, being a renewable source, will be available for future generations.

Bottom—Approaching storm, Mason County.
Right top—Double exposed woodland image.
Bottom right—Waterfalls on Laurel Creek, Fayette County.

SMOKE HOLE REGION

SMOKE HOLE IS AN AREA OF THE MONONGA-HELA NATIONAL FOREST LOCATED ON THE NORTH FORK OF THE SOUTH BRANCH OF THE POTOMAC RIVER. THE RIVER PLUNGES TURBULENTLY THROUGH A rugged canyon for a number of miles. There are numerous caves in the canyon walls and mountainside emitting cool air which forms a mist when it mixes with the moist warmer air from the river's surface. This is one explanation for the derivation of the name Smoke Hole. Local lore claims the name comes from the fact that Indians used the caves for smoking meat. The caves were also popular with moonshiners and the fires under their stills must have caused smoke.

The region is noted for its rugged mountain beauty, particularly from Cave Mountain. The once almost inaccessible area has now been developed to a point where many pursuits may be enjoyed. White water paddling through the turbulent gorge is popular, offering both action and beauty. Fishing has been a rewarding sport for many years. Camping, cave exploration, and bird study are popular. The canyon might be called a geologist's laboratory, particularly the strata of Eagle Rock which illustrates the earth's convulsive pressures that formed the mountains many years ago. Eagle Rock was named for William Eagle, a Revolutionary War veteran who settled in the Smoke Hole area and is buried near the cliff bearing his name. Botany of the region is diverse and supports a wide variety of wild flowers.

Top—Fall oak leaves.
Right—South Branch of the Potomac River flows through the Smoke Hole Canyon.
Bottom—Eagle Rock.

Top right—Portrait of Pearl S. Buck by artist Marj Teague.
Top—Sunset rays reflect on the Sydenstricker House.
Bottom right—Sydenstricker family Bible.

PEARL BUCK'S BIRTHPLACE

WEST VIRGINIA LISTS ITS MANY ILLUSTRIOUS NATIVES HIGH AMONG HER ASSETS. PEARL S. BUCK, NOTED AUTHOR AND HUMANITARIAN, CERTAINLY QUALIfies for a position at the top of the list. Her writings have been acclaimed throughout the world and her more than 100 books have been translated in over 50 languages. She was awarded the Nobel Prize for literature in 1938—the first American woman to be so honored.

In her many humanitarian endeavors, Pearl Buck is well known for her work in improving the lot of disadvantaged children. She founded Welcome House Incorporated, in 1949 to promote adoption of mixed Asian-American parentage children. The Pearl S. Buck Foundation was organized in 1964 for a similar purpose, particularly assisting children in their native lands.

Pearl Buck died at the age of 80 on March 6, 1973.

The Sydenstricker House at Hillsboro, West Virginia, is the birthplace of Pearl Buck. It was the ancestral home of her father. The property, which is on the National Register of Historic Places, was purchased by the farsighted West Virginia Federation of Women's Clubs. They organized the Pearl S. Buck Birthplace Foundation, Incorporated, for purposes of administration in 1966. Restoration has proceeded under sponsorship of the Federation Foundation and the United States Department of the Interior, National Park Service.

Right—Shavers Fork south of Bemis.
Bottom—Cathedral Falls, Fayette County.

Poke berries.

Twin Falls pioneer farm during autumn.

TWIN
PIONEER

BY THE MIDDLE OF THE NINETEENTH CENTURY, THE PATTERN OF WEST VIRGINIA MOUNTAIN FARMS WAS WELL ESTABLISHED. THE MEAGER EXISTENCE OF COLONIAL TIMES HAD STEADILY IMproved until one could then expect the typical farm to have a house, barn, pigpen, smokehouse, corncrib, chicken house and any others found necessary. These would all be made of logs on stone foundations. Fields and garden plots were cleared and fenced, once again using logs split into rails.

Food was grown on the farm with corn and pork as major staples. Chickens, garden products, fruit and wild grown delicacies, such as berries and nuts, furnished variety. Hunting game served as recreation and when successful supplemented the diet.

The affluent farm family might boast some "store bought" cloth, but as a rule "linsey-woolsey" still prevailed. This coarse cloth was woven from (home grown) wool and flax fibers. The appearance of this fabric was usually improved by using natural dyes for color. Walnut hulls and pokeberries, to name a few, were popular.

As the family increased in size and the farm became more prosperous, the original log house would be expanded. If a sawmill were near, the original logs might be covered with a form of clapboard siding. Such was

Autumn leaves cover old stone wall.

FALLS FARM

the case of the Bower Farm, a part of the present Twin Falls State Park area. The farm buildings were scheduled to be razed in order to prepare the area for park use. Morris "Smokey" Harsh, Twin Falls Park Superintendent at the time, uncovered the original log house and barn while tearing down the structures. He conceived the idea of restoring the original farm as a tourist attraction. His vision and efforts have been successful. All of the buildings have been reconstructed using original timbers from similar buildings of the area. It is complete even to a hand hewn picket fence around the house and chickens in the yard.

Left—Double image of autumn dogwood leaves and waterfall at Cacapon State Park.
Top—Bluestone River, Summers County.

Top—Icicles
Left—Cathedral State Park in Preston County.
Bottom—Sunrise on Opequon Creek in Berkeley County.

WINTER

WHEELING— FIRST CAPITAL

A MAJORITY OF THE PEOPLE LIVING IN THE WESTERN COUNTIES OF VIRGINIA DURING THE TRAGIC CIVIL WAR ERA DISAGREED WITH THE EASTERN COUNTIES ABOUT SECESSION FROM THE UNION. During 1861 opposition to secession increased to a point in the western counties wherein a group of citizens met on June 20, 1861 and adopted a Declaration of Independence from Virginia. Two years later, President Lincoln recognized the new State of West Virginia.

In 1851 the United States Congress designated Wheeling (then Virginia) a Port of Entry, and in 1869 a federal building to house the custom house, post office and federal court was completed. This building was used by the new government as the first West Virginia State Capitol. After the state capital was moved to Charleston, the building served a variety of uses, both governmental and commercial.

Public pride in our state's early history has resulted in a program of restoration of the building to its original 1863 condition. The office of Francis H. Pierpont, first West Virginia Governor, as well as the court room, is an excellent example of the skill and faithfulness with which restoration is done. It is easy to imagine Christmas celebrations at that time. The practice of decorating with evergreens and holly was popular in the 1860's as it still is today.

Right—Holly berries.
Bottom—Independence Hall.

Left—Governor Pierpont's Office (1861-63).
Bottom—Court room, state of West Virginia's birthplace.

Top left—The American and West Virginia flags grace the state capitol.
Top right—Looking up into the capitol dome.
Following overleaf—Aerial winter view of the capitol complex.
Bottom left—Night scene of the Science and Culture Center.
Bottom right—Foyer in the Governor's Mansion.

CAPITOL COMPLEX

THE WEST VIRGINIA STATE CAPITOL COMPLEX IS GENERALLY RECOGNIZED AS ONE OF THE MORE BEAUTIFUL IN THE NATION, AND IS A FITTING SUPPLEMENT TO THE OVERALL GRANDEUR OF OUR STATE. In 1974 a portion of the Complex, which includes the Capitol Building, grounds and Executive Mansion, was placed in the National Register of Historic Places. This was in tribute to its architectural and historical significance.

Historically, West Virginia's Capital had a turbulent beginning. The State Capital originated in Wheeling about the time of the proclamation of statehood by President Abraham Lincoln in 1863. Seven years later the Legislature voted to move it to Charleston. After only five years the Legislature voted in 1875 to move back to Wheeling. Dissatisfaction with the Wheeling site surfaced again and two years later, in 1877, the Legislature left the choice to the public and by popular vote Charleston was selected.

The present Capitol Building was dedicated by Governor William G. Conley on June 20, 1932. Structurally the building is made of limestone over a steel frame with most of the interior finished in marble. Several statistics will tend to illustrate the immense size of the structure. The building houses some 330 rooms and has more than 14 acres of floor space. The prominent dome is 293 feet high, exceeding that of the United States Capitol by five feet.

Five other major buildings complete the Complex: Executive Mansion, Science and Culture Center and three office buildings.

The Executive Mansion is a graceful Georgian colonial structure of red brick and white cornices, columns and trim. It faces the Kanawha River. The spacious interior is divided into state and private quarters. The first floor, with the exception of the kitchen and family dining room, is essentially for state functions. These are also available to the public at scheduled times. The second floor is reserved for a governor's family.

The Science and Culture Center completed in 1976 is dedicated to documenting, preserving and promoting West Virginia history, culture and science. It requires a number of visits and hours to adequately study the many endeavors housed in this one building. Natives can trace their roots through the museum or the vast library facilities. Arts and crafts are promoted through display and sale on a non-profit basis. A modern, fully equipped theatre seating 500 caters to a full range of cultural pursuits on a free-ticket policy.

For the first time, it is possible to see, in one place, much of what makes up West Virginia and its people.

115

MONONGAHELA

Footprints on top of Spruce Knob in the Monongahela National Forest mark the top of West Virginia at 4862 feet, the highest point in the state.

THE MONONGAHELA NATIONAL FOREST, CONSISTING OF 280,000 ACRES OF THE ALLEGHENY MOUNTAIN RANGE, LIES WHOLLY WITHIN WEST VIRGINIA. WE SHARE THE THOMAS JEFFERSON AND George Washington National Forests with our neighbor Virginia.

The concept of national forests developed early in the 20th century as a means of modifying disastrous floods that were plaguing the nation. The Monongahela National Forest in conjunction with retention reservoirs eases the threat to the Ohio Valley drainage basin. In addition to flood control the principle of comprehensive management so as to best serve the public's needs is practiced.

Equitable management of this vast area has a number of facets. Financial income is derived from the harvesting of mature timber and leasing of grazing land.

NATIONAL FOREST

The major emphasis, however, is placed on recreational sites serving camping, fishing, hunting, backpacking, picnicking and swimming or whatever else the outdoor enthusiast might desire. This wide variety of outdoor pursuits is designed to range from the needs of the picnickers to those of the sophisticated trailer camper or the rugged hiker carrying all his gear on his back.

It has been said that the Monongahela National Forest is about a half a day's drive from a third of the nation's population. This coupled with the fact that the forest is in West Virginia makes our state a host to a good share of the nation.

Top—Sinks of Gandy Cave, Randolph County.
Left—Small mountain stream in Blackwater Falls State Park, Tucker County.
Bottom—Canaan Valley State Park Ski Area.

A view of Seneca Rocks along Seneca Creek in the Monongahela National Forest.

SENECA ROCKS

SENECA ROCKS, AN IMPOSING PART OF THE SPRUCE KNOB–SENECA ROCKS NATIONAL RECREATIONAL AREA WITHIN THE MONONGAHELA NATIONAL FOREST, IS NOTED FOR BEAUTY, HISTORY AND LEGend. Beauty of the area is a combination of things. The most spectacular is the almost vertical rock walls towering nearly 1000 feet above the confluence of Seneca Creek and the North Fork of the South Branch of the Potomac River. Geologists tell us that many millions of years ago tremendous earth pressures caused an upheaval of the tuscarora sandstone, thus forming the Appalachian Mountains. Erosion has reduced these once mighty mountains and in places more resistant strata, such as Seneca Rocks, remain. In geological time, these rocks will also disintegrate into grains of sand and perhaps again form sandstone as they originally did. The mountains enclosing Seneca Rocks and the North Fork Valley lend a softening quality to a scene that in itself might be harsh.

During World War II the armed forces' 10th Mountaineer Division trained here. Their climbing exercises required driving so many pitons in the rock face (special spikes driven into crevices) that the term "face of 1000 pitons" has been commonly applied. Climbing as a peacetime sport has increased in popularity over the years and Seneca Rocks has become popular. Many enthusiasts consider these rocks to be one of the most difficult and challenging climbs in the East.

Seneca Rocks are named for the Seneca Indians initially inhabiting the area and herein arises a romantic legend. Princess Snowbird, beautiful daughter of Chief Bald Eagle, chose a challenging method of selecting a husband. During her youth she developed climbing skills which enabled her to reach the summit of Seneca Rocks. When her time came to marry, she declared that she would climb the rocks and the first brave to reach her at the top would be her husband. A number of young men started but only one succeeded. The rest either turned back or fell to their deaths. Princess Snowbird must have been a remarkable climber, exceeding any of the men. The cliffhanger tale has it that the winning suitor slipped and nearly fell to his death during the last few feet of the climb, but Princess Snowbird grabbed his hand and pulled him to safety.

Left—Five Mile Creek in Mason County creates ice-cracked pattern.
Top—Sunset at 10 degrees below zero in Blackwater Falls State Park.

123

COVERED BRIDGES

COVERED BRIDGES, LIKE THE HORSE AND BUGGY, ARE A ROMANTIC LINK TO THE RECENT PAST. WE ARE FORTUNATE IN WEST VIRGINIA IN THAT SOME OF THESE BRIDGES STILL EXIST AND ARE IN use. Tales have come down to us over the years of many things happening in these structures other than transportation over a stream. A swain was apt to stop his horse and buggy for a bit of romance, and it often took the place of the drugstore as a young people's hangout. Vendors posted their handbills inside out of the weather, and on the grim side, highwaymen found the dark shadows a good place to commit their crimes.

The need for bridges kept pace with America's growth and early crude structures gave way to more sophisticated needs. Bridge builders were limited to using wood and stone, the materials at hand. A high degree of engineering skill is evident in the way wooden beams were used to form arches and trusses for maximum strength. The often told tale of Lemuel Chenoweth, master bridge builder of the area, serves to illustrate. The Virginia Board of Public Works advertised for bids to build bridges on the Staunton to Parkersburg turnpike. Mr. Chenoweth assembled a wooden model before the commissioners. It was small enough for the parts to have been carried over the mountain on horseback. He suspended his model across two chairs and walked its length. He won the bid and subsequently built a number of bridges in what is now West Virginia; the Philippi covered bridge being one still in use today.

Inasmuch as the bridge superstructures were of wood, weather deterioration of the vital support beams was a problem. Lacking today's paints and preservatives, the logical move was enclosure, thus the covered bridge.

Of the more than fifty covered bridges that once spanned West Virginia streams, only a few now remain. Demise of the structures was due to flood, fire, demolition for building modern bridges and neglect. The following covered bridges still exist in West Virginia:

BARBOUR COUNTY
Buckhannon River (at Carrollton)
Tygart River (at Philippi)
CABELL COUNTY
Mud Creek (at Milton)
GREENBRIER COUNTY
Milligan Creek (Northwest of Lewisburg)
Second Creek (at Hokes Mill)
HARRISON COUNTY
Ten Mile Creek (North of Maken)
Simpson Creek (at Hollen Mill)
Rooting Creek (South of Romines Mills)
JACKSON COUNTY
Left Fork Sandy Creek (Between Odaville and Sandyville)
Tug Fork (at Staats Mill)
LEWIS COUNTY
Right Fork of West Fork River (South of Walkersville)
MARION COUNTY
Paw Paw Creek (at Grant Town)
Buffalo Creek (at Barrackville)
MONROE COUNTY
Laural Creek (Near Lillydale)
6 miles South of Union (at St. John's Church)
MONONGALIA COUNTY
Dents Run (North of Laurel Point)
POCAHONTAS COUNTY
Locust Creek (Near Hillsboro)
WETZEL COUNTY
Fish Creek (Near Hundred)

Covered bridge spans Mud River at Milton.

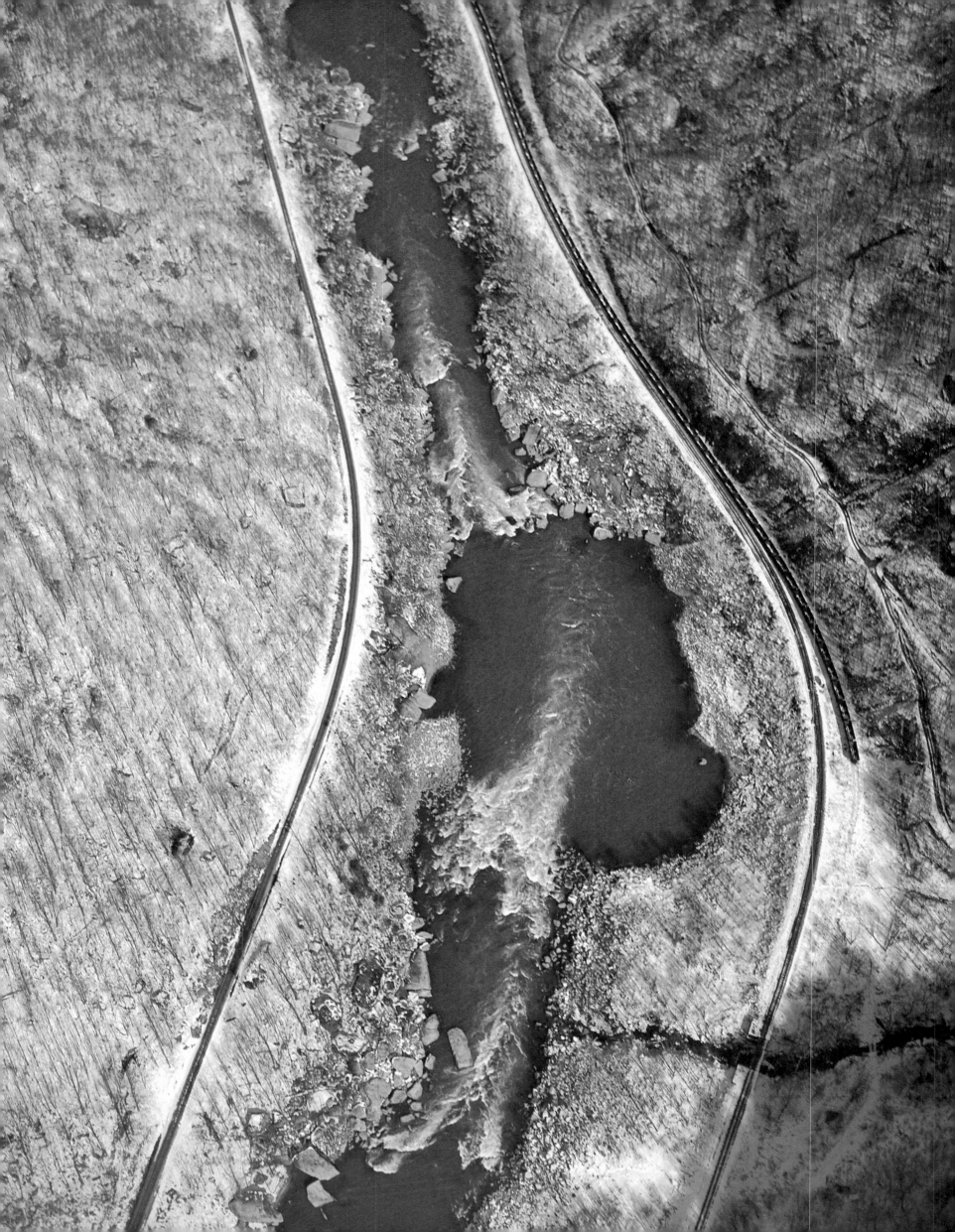

Left—Aerial view of Keeney Creek rapids on New River.
Bottom—Aerial winter scene of Stephens Lake.

Cardinal, the state bird, perches on a snowy pine branch.